Chasing My Passion and My Calling

LORNA RAMIREZ

First published in Australia 2015
This edition published 2018
Copyright © Lorna Ramirez 2015
Cover design, typesetting: Working Type Studio, Melbourne

The right of Lorna Ramirez to be identified as the Author of the Work has been asserted in accordance with the Copyright, Designs and Patents Act 1988.

All rights reserved. No part of this publication may be reproduced, stored in a retrieval system, or transmitted, in any form or by any means without the prior written permission of the publisher, nor be otherwise circulated in any form of binding or cover other than that in which it is published and without a similar condition being imposed on the subsequent purchaser.

Ramirez, Lorna
Chasing my Passion and My Calling
ISBN (pbk): 978-0-6482130-4-8
ISBN (ebook): 978-0-6482130-5-5
pp118

Sources of Information:

Footscray Historical Society

Heritage Place Victoria, Heritage Overlay no. HO135, Hermes number 35583, File Number PL-HE/03/0929

About the Author

Lorna Ramirez was born, raised and educated in Manila in the Philippines, attaining a degree in Chemical Engineering and working as a laboratory manager in a textiles company.

In 1977, with her husband and her son and daughter she migrated to Australia. She worked as a laboratory technician and a chemist in Australia, only retiring in the year 2000 to care for her first grandchild.

Lorna Ramirez has travelled extensively, gaining much from her interactions with people all over the world and building a strong foundation for her philosophies about life.

She loves gardening, cooking and reading and playing the piano. She is also interested in the Stock Exchange. Throughout her life Lorna Ramirez, a woman of faith, has been a wise observer of human behaviour and has collected her many wisdoms and observations.

Her book *My Innermost Thoughts — The Realities of Life* was published in mid-2014.

Acknowledgements

Sincere thanks to Renalyn Cerezo and Alyssa Cary for typing my manuscripts and to Alyssa for doing the illustrations on verses 1,4,5,6 in Chapter IX in this book, and also to Footscray Historical Society for helping me with my research.

To

To my loving husband — Claro
Gorgeous grandchildren — Alyssa and Amelia
My children and their partners
Carlo and Marie
Maritess and Steven

Contents

PREFACE 1

PROLOGUE 3

CHAPTER I — *Coming to Australia, New Life* 5

CHAPTER II — *Midway Hostel* 9

CHAPTER III — *Life after Hostel* 21

CHAPTER IV — *Turning Point* 27

CHAPTER V — *Reborn* 31

CHAPTER VI — *Aftermath* 35

CHAPTER VII — *Chasing the Dream* 39

CHAPTER VIII — *The Connection* 43

CHAPTER IX — *Inspirational Messages* 49

Preface

Based on true events, this book was written to give the readers a glimpse of, and insight into, the earlier migrants of 1977 who chose Australia as their adopted country.

Names of the characters in this story have been changed to protect their identities.

This book describes how the migrants were given assistance by the government and their lives and experiences in the Midway Hostel in Maribyrnong, now known as the Student Village.

Migrants' children should embrace this legacy left to them by their parents. This must-read book will inform them of the trials and triumphs their parents experienced as newcomers to this land.

It is a book that may help us understand that life is a miracle, and all of us have a mission or calling and it is up to us to find it!

All inspirational messages are the original work of the author and any similarity to other works is purely coincidental.

Lorna Ramirez

Prologue

Once we have gone through

Trials and tribulations

The more we appreciate

The real essence

Of what life is all about

Then we start to learn more

Of our inner selves

And the people around us

Each one of us has a cross to carry

It depends on how we will be able

To go through each endeavour that

Crosses our path

I believe it is not just about living our lives

But it is all about *how* we live

Our lives here on earth

I also do believe the reason

I am here is because I do have

A calling, a mission to be fulfilled

My name is Evelyn Valdez and

Here is my story...

Chapter 1

Coming to Australia
(The New Life)

It was raining heavily on that night of the 31st of August 1977 as we drove to the airport for a new life in Australia. Sadness could be seen on both my husband's and my parents' faces. We reached the airport an hour early, travelling at night. When it was time to go, tears flowed from my eyes as I kissed all of them goodbye. Our parents hugged the kids. I could feel their pain: they love their grandchildren, but they had to let them go.

My husband Chris is an electrician and we were granted a family-assisted program to migrate to Australia.

I have two kids, Brandon, aged 9, and Michelle, aged 5. The kids and I were all excited. This was our first flight in an airplane.

It took us an eight-hour journey from Manila to Australia, but for me, it seemed forever. I had mixed emotions — excited but scared. I didn't know what to expect, going to another country with a different culture and no relatives and friends. It was a huge gamble at that time.

We arrived at the Melbourne Airport on the morning of 1st September, 1977. The weather was sunny, yet chilly, a stark contrast from the tropical weather back home.

We were met by the government staff, who led us to a waiting cab.

On the way to our destination, we were all overwhelmed by what we saw: big open spaces, beautiful very green scenery — and the air smelled very fresh. I knew at that moment we had made the right decision.

Chapter II

Midway Hostel

We reached our destination, the Midway Hostel at Hampstead Road, Maidstone, for newly arrived migrants, now known as the Student Village.

The Midway Hostel complex was comprised of two-storey accommodation buildings clustered into six groups. Also included were four laundry buildings, an English Language school, a child care centre with grassed play areas and sandpit and a communal dining hall, where food was provided for breakfast, lunch and dinner.

It also included scattered rockeries set in the polygonal concrete-paved island. Between each pavilion in the ground floor walkway was a small telephone for residents to keep in contact with their home countries. A landscape garden was created inside the ring, which was planted with trees and shrubs.

A friendly staff member took us to an interview room where he helped and guided us with our applications for Medicare, children's allowance and unemployment allowance.

They explained to us that the board and lodging were free and once we found a job, we could have the option to stay for a few months but this time giving a contribution.

After the interview, they took us to a two-bedroom unit (BemJ was the name of the unit). It had a bathroom but no kitchen, as no cooking was allowed. Food was provided at the communal or dining hall.

My son Brandon said, "Mum, we have a bathtub. Are we rich now?"

I said, "No son. They all have bathtubs in Australia. We still have to work hard to be comfortable."

He smiled and said, "I think I will love to stay in Australia."

Foods were in abundance, complete with main dishes, salads galore and different varieties of veggies and desserts. Our sheets were washed weekly for us.

We had a supply of fresh milk and fruit every afternoon. For our spiritual needs, Sunday mass was given and performed at the hostel. A school bus took migrant children to either Catholic or public schools in the area and dropped them back at the hostel.

Within two weeks at the hostel, Chris and I had jobs. I worked as a technician in the carpet industry and Chris worked as an electrical maintenance officer in the manufacturing industry. We opted to stay for another two months.

Filipino families bonded together really well. Everyone was called Tita (auntie) and Tito (uncle) by the kids.

We were the first Filipino migrant family staying in the hostel to own a brand new car. It was a yellow two-door Toyota sedan, which cost only $6,200.00. (Registration number IYE-406.) When we drove it into the hostel grounds, everyone wanted a ride. It was a small car and yet nine people managed to squeeze themselves into that car, mostly kids. However, we just drove around within the compound.

The yellow car was always used and borrowed for hospital and other emergencies.

Amongst Filipino migrants, our relationships with each other were quite remarkable as we tried to hold on to one another for strength and security — especially as we were in this new country where we had no families and friends.

There were several communal laundry facilities at the hostel and, of course, they became meeting places for activities and gossiping, mainly for women. In these we interacted with one another and we came to know different races and cultures.

Every Sunday, the nuns or sisters were responsible for providing a mass service, which was attended by Catholics, Protestants, and others. The majority of Filipinos were Catholic, so after mass we would catch up with one another while the kids enjoyed themselves playing.

Indeed it seemed to be paradise, but we still missed our loved ones back home. But it was for the sake of our kids' futures that we had to do this.

We all looked forward to 'Trash and Treasure' shopping after

Chapter II

Sunday lunch. It could be found in front of the Highpoint Shopping Centre back then; but now the centre is full of retail stores such as Harvey Norman, Fantastic Furniture, Captain Snooze and others and there is no need for Trash and Treasure stalls.

During the year 1977 there were more migrants coming from non-English speaking countries, such as Greece, Spain, Yugoslavia, and South America. Since the hostel had a communal hall, we were not allowed to cook in our unit. Although the food was in abundance at the hostel, we Filipinos had a craving for Filipino dishes. It was the first time that we tasted lamb, rabbit, mutton, or veal. We normally had pork, chicken or beef back at home.

The average loaf of bread was only 48 cents and the yearly wage was $9000 per annum. The latest technology was a cassette, (the tablet of today's era).

Indeed year 1977 was so special for me. It was a year where we were given a chance to start a new life in this beautiful paradise called Australia.

Thanks to the generosity of some Filipino families that lived outside the hostel in Melbourne we were invited to lunch and dinner on weekends. Much to our delight, we had a chance to savour our Filipino dishes again.

In the hostel, for those who were already working, after dinner at the communal hall we filled in a form to order pre-packed lunches for work: so many cold cuts and roasts from which to choose. Then after breakfast the next day we collected our pre-packed lunch, and went to work.

I vividly remember my first encounter with Vegemite

spread. Intrigued by its unusual name, I tried it in my prepacked lunch for work.

Looking forward to it, and really hungry at lunch break, I grabbed my lunch, very eager to have a taste of my Vegemite sandwich. One bite of it and there was an explosion of the most bitter, unusual taste that I have ever experienced. I rushed to the toilet to spit it out. It was so lucky that I had other sandwiches with different fillings to satisfy my hunger. Now, Vegemite is my favourite spread.

At the hostel, a frail elderly sister or nun assisted us, the new migrants, for all our spiritual needs. As well, she gave us thick clothing and cardigans for surviving cold nights or weather in Melbourne. She was such a nice and sweet lady, who was loved by all residents at the hostel.

Even our kids had to adapt to the new environment. My son Brandon was nine and Michelle was five years old.

Michelle had developed a urinary infection because she was too scared to ask for permission in class to go to the toilet. She tried to hold it in for the whole day. That was the first time we went to the Western General Hospital. She was treated and given antibiotics.

The second time I took the kids to the emergency room was when both of them vomited during the night. I was so shaken. Doctors found that it was probably just a virus; nothing serious.

We were all adjusting, but thanks to the support and assistance from the Australian government, it became easier for us to be a part of our new country.

Our first New Year celebration while we are at the hostel was an unforgettable experience.

The Payos, Pascos, and our families decided to spend the New Year's celebration at the flat of friends, Mr and Mrs Thor Brizwell, who, at that time, lived in a Churchill Avenue, Braybrook flat.

The ladies spent the whole afternoon at the flat cooking and preparing to greet our first New Year in Australia.

Around nine o'clock at night, our husbands said to us, "Listen, we have to go and help Ben fix his car. It is stranded or stuck near the corner of Ashley and Churchill, in Braybrook." Of course we said yes and Emy said, "It's only nine o'clock; still early before we greet the New Year." So, Chris, Thor and Gammy took off.

It was nearing midnight with still no sign of our husbands, and Emy said, "If they are fixing the car why was Thor wearing his best shirt, and why did he have a shower this afternoon and smell nice?"

"You are right, Emy," I said. "Even Chris is wearing his best shirt and his shoes were polished."

"You're right. Ben just dropped us here and said he would be coming later," Fe, Ben's wife, said.

We all agreed that something was not right so we decided to go to the place where the car was stuck.

It was almost midnight, dark with lots of drunks about, but we braved the night and walked to the place where they said the car was stranded. To our dismay there was no sign of our husbands or the red Morris car.

We went back to the flat, angry and furious. "They have tricked us," I said.

After arriving at the flats we went to Charlie, the neighbour, to ask for the whereabouts of our husbands. At first, he was reluctant to help us but after we persisted, he drove us to the Ascot Vale house. There was a 'bachelor' party being held, and with mostly Australian female friends!

We went inside and I will never forget the surprised look on our husbands' faces. I saw Chris sitting on the chair clapping his hands to the tune of the music. 'Mighty Thor', Ben and Gammy were all dancing with the Australian ladies. Their escapade was cut short.

They had a lot of explaining to do. Tears and emotions ran high. That was our very first New Year celebration in Australia.

During our stay at the hostel we bonded with Filipino families who became our extended families, even up to today. They were the Abera, Campos, Pasco, Lope, Brizwell and Payos families, and many more. Their children and grandchildren still interact and are friends with my own kids and grandchildren.

Most of the families I knew back then at the hostel have successful children. Some are now doctors, lawyers, graphic designers, chemists and accountants.

I believe we have already paid our dues to Australia by helping shape the country, but most of all by producing children that are responsible hardworking Australians — in our adopted beautiful country, Australia.

The Maribyrnong Migrant Hostel was one of several

With no families in Australia in 1977, we bonded together with new found friends, always camping together during week ends. Our life in 1977.

migrant hostels established in Melbourne. Before the year 1969 migrants were initially accommodated in prefabricated structures, predominately Nissen huts. The site included Nissen and Romney huts. Most of these huts were acquired from the British Ministry of Works, and some from private dealers. They were replaced with the construction of the Midway Hostel in 1969.

The assisted package scheme that we had was phased out

in 1982. The Commonwealth Accommodation And Catering Services LTD was sold in 1988 becoming Allied Food Services. The hostel was closed, and the site was taken over in 1989 by the Footscray Institute of Technology, to be used as student accommodation.

As migrants from 1977, we all have shared unforgettable memories from when we lived at Midway Hostel.

Back home in the Philippines we don't use the sign 'No Standing' as it is used in Australia, relating to cars. Whenever we saw the sign, we Filipinos moved away interpreting it literally that one was not allowed to stand in that spot. We also learned different colloquial language or slang, such as biro for ballpoint pen, lift for elevator, brolly for umbrella, snag for sausage, and footpath for sidewalk. The list goes on and on.

After coming to Australia in 1977, we found Christmas and New Year celebrations were a little bit laid back. This added more to the loneliness we felt, and made us miss our loved ones left behind. One of the many ways extended families and friends could alleviate our grief and loneliness was to congregate, share food at different celebrations and exchange gifts at Christmas parties.

In today's environment, Christmas and New Year celebrations are more alive and vibrant.

Indeed, I would say, the former Maribyrnong Migrant Hostel is of historical significance and origin, for its association with post-World War Two migrants, who contributed to the growth of the Australian multicultural society.

Our house is just a few kilometres from the Midway Hostel. Each time I pass by the building, a feeling of sadness, joy, and mixed emotions comes to me. But it always puts a smile on my face. Those unforgettable memories, bad ones but mostly good ones, are still in my mind. Our lives and future were shaped and started in this building.

We found and came to know beautiful wonderful families, and friendships that developed have passed the test of time.

Of course, our own family had grown bigger; we now have a son-and daughters-in-law and grandchildren, but we still connect and interact with one another. All of this started in this building, the Midway Hostel.

Friends that last forever

And loving families

These are priceless, worth more

Than the riches of the world

They give us the reason

That life is worth living

Chapter III

Life after Hostel

We moved to a two-bedroom flat (apartment) in Dunlop Street, Maribyrnong, walking distance from St Margaret Primary Catholic School.

Since both of us were working, Brandon learned at the early age of nine years old to look after his younger sister Michelle, who was five years old. They walked by themselves to school and home. At that time we didn't worry about children being abducted. We were also lucky to have, beside our flat, a Filipino neighbour, who helped us look after the kids.

My heart bled each time I went to work leaving my kids but we had no choice as we had to work.

Life in Australia in 1977 was so different. Shops and banks were open five days a week and on Friday were also open up to 9:00pm. Milk bars (local general stores) were popular in each suburb. We don't see many of these around today. We

would barely see a soul when we went to the city during weekends. However, this was compensated for by the fact that almost every weekend, with extended families and friends, we went to different camping areas in Victoria — fishing, bush walking and just relaxing.

This was our first snow experience, kids were so excited.

The kids loved interacting with other kids of the extended families and enjoying the camping experience. With no computers and modern technologies then, they appreciated more the beauty of nature and each other's company.

These are my yesteryear memories I will never forget and that will always put a smile on my face.

The Highpoint West mall was not very big compared with how huge it is to today. Opposite, across the road from the mall, was the vacant lot (at present, different retail establishments are located there), where the Trash and Treasure stalls I spoke of earlier were held every weekend. It was a paradise to migrants, just walking distance from Midway Hostel. Those days you could find real treasures such as nice silver cutlery, kitchen equipment and gadgets.

At night, the vacant lot was used as a Drive-in Cinema, very popular at that time. Today, Melbourne has only three Drive-in Cinemas.

In the 70s, becoming an Australian citizen was a lot easier. You had to be a permanent resident in Australia for two years with good moral character and the ability to speak and understand English, but it was not necessary to read and write English.

Throughout the years, we managed to pull through each challenge we had. After two years we became Australian citizens. We then moved to our very first house in East Keilor — near transport and a Catholic school. Then, as the kids had grown up, we moved to a bigger place at Avondale Heights, where we live at present.

Years passed: the children both grew up and finished their college degrees. Brandon married Diana. Michelle married Edward and was blessed with two gorgeous daughters, Simone and Kaitlin.

Chris and I were both retired, enjoying each other's company and the remaining years of our lives. We travelled extensively around the world, and went to different breathtaking places in Australia. I thought it would never end until one day, the day I won't forget, something happened...

This was our first car, first flat and my oldest son aged 9 in Australia.

Chapter IV

Turning Point

May 16, 2010

Every Sunday morning, as often as possible, we attended Mass in our community Parish church. Today's Sunday was no different. It was a bright sunny day. Chris and I decided to take a walk after Mass in the nearby Tea Garden Park opposite our house. We hurriedly went home and changed into our walking gear.

    I do love walking with Chris, admiring those majestic trees along the river banks of the Maribyrnong River that have been there for hundreds of years, and the natural rock formations of different shapes, sizes and colours along the walking path. Truly feasts for our eyes.

    A peaceful sanctuary within bustling municipalities, the

Maribyrnong River and valley offer spaces for relaxing and recreation. At times we can see wild life such as birds, rabbit, bats, insects, reptiles, mammals and frogs.

The Tea Garden is complete with barbeque facilities and a playground. I could hear children's laughter and screaming as I reminisced about those days when our kids were young. They loved this place. Even today, people come here to the Tea Garden for fishing, walking, jogging, bird observing and cycling. There is an activity for everyone.

Feeling tired after walking for a few hours, I said, "Chris, I'm tired. I've had enough. Let's start walking home."

Chris replied, "Okay, we will head home and rest."

It was almost noon, so I prepared our lunch, then rested and watched TV. Suddenly I felt an intense pain at the back of my abdomen, spreading to my groin and leg. I screamed with pain.

Chris rushed from the bedroom into the family room, where he saw me in pain. He said, "What's wrong, Honey? I will call Triple O."

My face was pale; then I felt blood coming from my behind. I was bleeding heavily. Fortunately, an ambulance came at once. It drove me to Western Hospital in Footscray.

I was given a blood transfusion, subjected to a CT scan that found out I had an intestinal rupture of a blood vessel — an abdominal aneurysm.

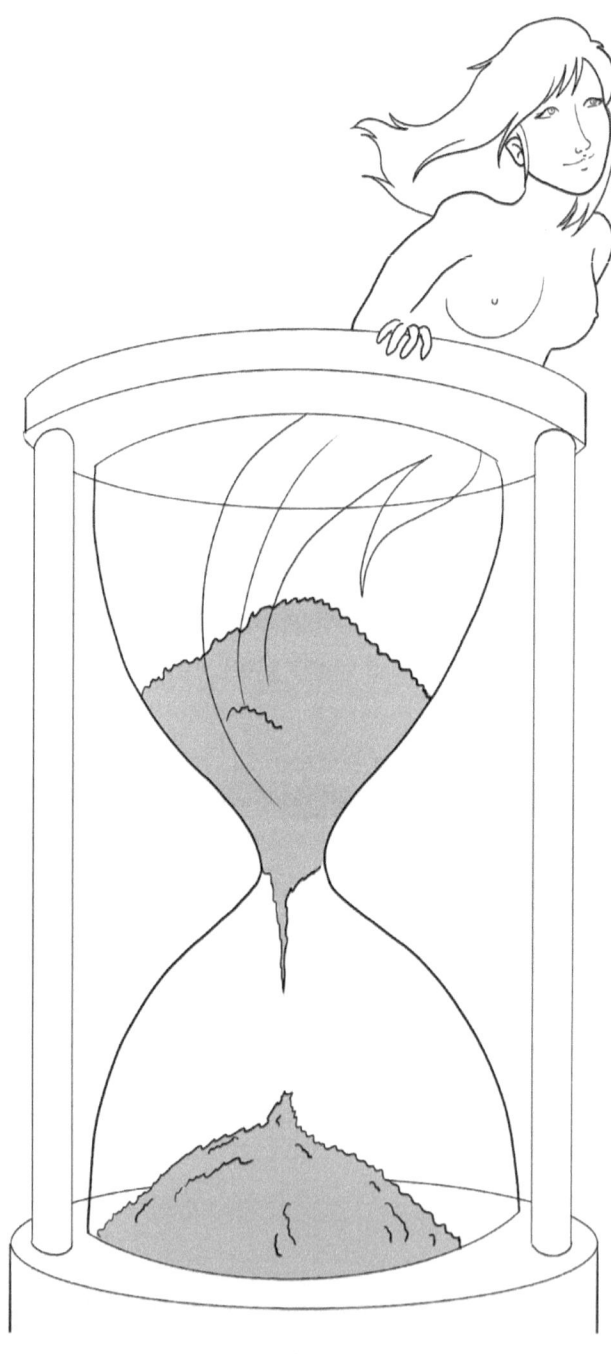

Chapter V

Reborn

At the theatre, regional anesthesia was given, affecting only the lower half of my body. Thus I was awake throughout the procedure. The procedure is called aneurysm embolisation, a risky one. It could have damaged the bowel and surrounding blood vessels and I could have bled to death.

A catheter was placed through a small incision in my groin up to the location of the ruptured blood vessel. A platinum coil was pushed through into exact position at the ruptured vessel to block and stop the bleeding — as long as the stent was properly placed. The whole procedure can take almost four hours.

After more than three hours of surgery, I felt coldness, beginning at my feet, envelop my whole body. It seemed as though the world had stood still and that I had travelled through time.

Serenity, complete peace, calmness — I experienced all of these. Then I saw beautiful rows of flowers, their fragrances greeting my senses. My whole body was feeling light as if I was walking in cloud. My surroundings were white.

At the far end, I could visualise a tunnel and at the end of a tunnel a striking, glittering brightness that almost blinded my eyes, a vision I could not comprehend and explain. I would have liked to have gone inside but my mind was saying no.

Slowly I walked to the tunnel but at the moment I tried to step inside, the door shut.

Then I woke up and heard the nurse saying, "Mrs Valdez, stay with us. Open your eyes."

She kept doing a tender slap on my face. She said urgently, "Doc, the blood pressure is at a dangerous level; even the heartbeat and pulse are low."

The doctor said, "Only a few seconds more...I think I have done it well. Let's hope no complications happen."

The procedure lasted almost four hours. I had used so many litres of blood that it seemed that my entire blood must have been replenished by new blood. Then they moved me to the recovery room.

After a few hours I was moved into my room. My children and their partners, grandchildren, my sister Violy — and a beautiful smile from my hubby Chris — greeted me as I entered the room. So nice to see all my family after that ordeal. I did not tell them anything that had happened in the theatre.

Chapter V

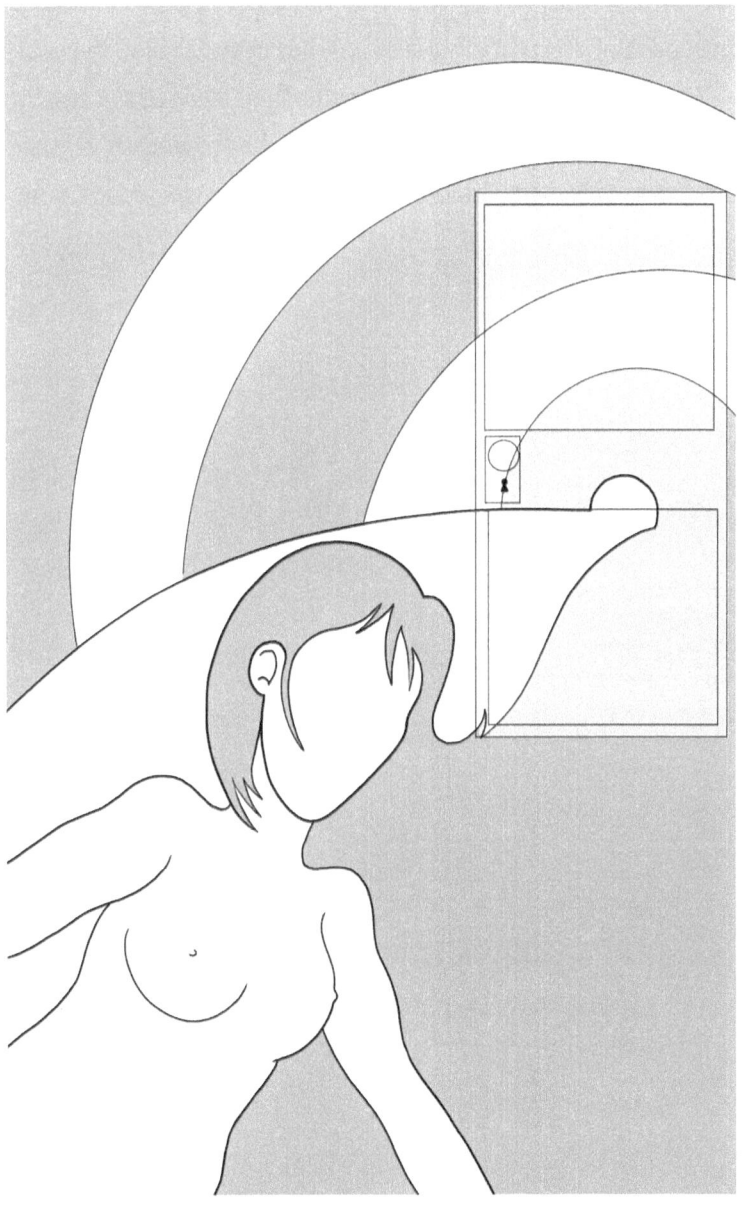

The following day the surgeon visited me in my room and said, "I am happy with the outcome. According to the scan, the coil was successfully placed at the ruptured blood vessel."

I stayed in the hospital for another fourteen days for further observation. The doctors were happy with my recovery. I was released. Chris picked me up and we drove home.

Chapter VI

Aftermath

Months passed. I was doing well, full of energy and back to my routine. I was even more passionate about playing classical piano pieces, gardening and cooking. It was Father's Day; all of my family was at my place. I was busy cooking but I always treasured the special moments to be with loved ones.

At this time I asked Michelle, my daughter, to sign me up on Facebook. She laughed and said, "Mum, you hate writing and besides Facebook is only for young ones."

With my persistence, she obliged. That was the start of my writing; I surprised myself that I could write; I didn't know where my thoughts and ideas were coming from. Each time I was at my computer, I started writing poems, inspirational messages and quotes, all based on my strong beliefs and convictions. Never in my wildest dreams did I imagine I would be able to do it.

Soon I received special messages from Facebook friends saying that they loved my messages, and a few people even began asking me for advice and opinions about their personal problems.

My passion for playing, especially classical piano pieces, intensified. I started playing music by Chopin, Franz Liszt and Mozart, to name a few.

Chris could see the change in me, and one day at the breakfast table he asked, "Evelyn, what's got into you? You have started having an interest in writing, which I know you have always hated. Also, before, you were not keen about sending birthday or Christmas cards to our friends and relatives. I have not heard you play for three decades — since we married. But now you start tickling the ivory keys. What has happened?"

I replied, "I don't have any explanation, Chris. I just feel my passion for writing and music in my heart."

He responded, "I think there is something that has happened to trigger your enthusiasm."

I said, "I can't think of anything else, Chris, except that I was hospitalised for an abdominal aneurysm."

Chris laughed and said, "HA HA HA — you believe that? We believe in the modern era. You and your imagination."

As usual, that day, Chris was busy in the backyard. Most of the time I stayed inside, writing, cooking or playing the piano.

For almost one and a half years I kept on writing and accumulated lots of inspirational poems, messages, quotes and beliefs. Everything looking rosy; I couldn't have asked for anything else. I enjoyed the company of good friends Carmena, Elitah, Tess, Flora, Terra and my sister, Violy. We would always go out for lunch, theatres and the cinema and once in a while tried our luck at the casino."

With a loving husband, two successful children and two gorgeous grandchildren, life was indeed ideal and perfect. Until one day another ordeal in my life happened, on the 18th November, 2012.

Chris was beside me at our kitchen bench table while I was sorting out the groceries he had just bought. Suddenly I had double vision. I couldn't see anything and passed out for a few seconds. I found myself in the arms of Chris, which preventing me from falling and hitting my head on the floor. The ambulance was called and I was rushed to the Western General Hospital.

Tests were done including a CT scan of my brain. Everything was normal. So it was neither a stroke nor a heart attack. The last test they did was an MRI. The result confirmed that I had a congenital brain aneurysm. I was so lucky this time as the blood vessel in my brain did not rupture. It was only small so it was inoperable. I was given a blood thinning tablet to be taken each day. My doctor said, through healthy diet and the medication, everything would be controlled.

After this frightening episode, I decided to write a book to have a legacy for my family, friends and relations. Life is too short and no one knows what the future will bring.

Chapter VII

Chasing the Dream

A favourite quote from my first book:

>All of us have gone through
>
>Several steps in our lives
>
>Each step is a learning experience
>
>At the end it is nice to look back
>
>Not counting the years you have gone through
>
>But counting the special moments
>
>That you have been through

After my second ordeal, the more convinced I became that I had a mission or calling that needed to be fulfilled: to write an inspirational book that would touch and reach people as much as I could and which would spread the words of Love, Peace, Perseverance, Humility and above all, our Love for our God Almighty.

It was true indeed that experiences from the past years had even made me stronger and more determined to pursue and chase my dream. I was aware also of the difficulty of publishing a book. I was prepared to do whatever it took to fulfil my dream.

I started organising and accumulating all of my writings from Facebook, and my notes and scribbles. I found it daunting organising everything. It took me a few weeks to accomplish it.

Next the task was to have it typed. Diana, my daughter-in-law, typed the first few pages but became very busy with her work and couldn't do anymore. Fortunately, Rena, a daughter of a friend of mine, typed my manuscript.

My manuscript was sent to many publishers. Being an unknown author, I found it difficult. Several publishers rejected my work. Feeling disappointed and frustrated, I turned to my husband and said, "Chris, I don't think I will have a chance to pursue my dream."

Chris said, "Don't stop following your dream. Keep on trying. I know you will be able to make it."

This was typical of Chris, my very supportive husband, who was always giving me hope and encouragement about what I was doing.

Browsing through the internet, I came across a publishing

company. I rang them and Ken, the owner, answered the phone. He agreed to have a look at my manuscript.

Wasting no time, I sent my manuscript through email. A few weeks later, my enthusiasm and excitement were dampened. I'd received an email from the publisher that told me that they did not have any provision or placement for my manuscript.

I was devastated by the result, but this time I wouldn't accept no for an answer. So I rang Ken.

"Ken, I am not thinking of publishing my book commercially. I just want a legacy for my family and friends."

Ken replied, "Okay, I will send it to my editor and if she agrees, it will be published."

Two weeks passed; feeling nervous but hopeful, I received an email from Ken. The editor loved my manuscript and recommended it for publication.

I jumped with joy, ran to Chris, who was busy in our backyard, hugged him and screamed at the top of my voice: "Chris, at last, I will be an author!"

Chris said, "I am overjoyed and very happy for you, Evelyn. I've had faith always in you. I always knew you could do it."

The following week, Ken gave me a copy editor to work with. After the book editing, it was given to a book designer. For my book cover, Eddie, son-in-law of one of my friends, did my photo shoot. Then an illustrator did dozens of illustrations and it went back again to the book designer and typesetter.

By the middle of 2014, it was finally printed and published.

This is a book so close to my heart, written with honesty, simplicity and purity. All words came from my heart and soul.

Chapter VIII

The Connection

Finally, I received the first copy of the book mid-2014. Impressed with the book, I ordered two hundred copies.

The whole family was excited especially my grandkid Kaitlin, who said, "Wow, Grandma, this is the first time my name is in a book."

I said, "Of course, sweetie. This will not be the last time. More will be coming."

Then her eyes brightened and she gave me a hug.

I then organised two book launches at my place. All my family were involved in presentation and arrangement. My sister Violy brought several friends to attend my launches.

My son-in-law Edward suggested that I should have a launch in Bendigo, saying quite a few people would be interested in buying the book.

The following month, in the last week of August, my book was launched at Bendigo. My son-in-law's family and friends and all of my family were there to support me.

Bendigo is a major regional city of Victoria, Australia approximately 150 kilometres northwest of the state capital, Melbourne. It is the fourth largest inland city in Australia and the most populous city in the state.

I was excited and quite nervous about the event but it turned out to be successful. One of Edward's family friends invited me for afternoon tea. Of course, I said yes.

My book launch for 'My Innermost Thoughts — The Realities of Life'.

Brandon, Diana, Edward and Michelle headed home. Simone and Kaitlin stayed with us.

Edward's friends' place was beautiful. Emma and her husband George were a lovely couple and very friendly.

Rows of beautiful geranium, roses and begonias of different colours were planted in the front yard, mixed with native shrubs and trees. They had a big verandah at the back where we had our tea, biscuits and cakes.

The kids Kaitlin and Simone were playing football in the spacious backyard full of fruit trees, a veggie patch and again rows of beautiful roses and geraniums. Even the verandah was filled with hanging begonias of different colours. Chris and George were busy tackling politics, sports and other topics.

As I entered the front door of the house and I walked to the back verandah, I felt something — as if I knew this place. The smell, the surroundings, all seemed very familiar to me, as if I had been here in this place before.

Sitting at the huge verandah, having a cup of tea, Emma said, "I wish my daughter Tessa was here. For sure she would have loved your launch."

I asked, "Where is Tessa now?"

Tears started to fill Emma's eyes as she said, "She's gone four years ago in a car accident, 16th May, 2010 at 4:00pm."

I experienced goose bumps, cold shivers and a sensation of disbelief and shock. I could hardly breathe — that day I will always remember. May 16, 2010 at 4:00pm was when I had my near-death experience during my abdominal surgery.

Emma said, "What's wrong, Mrs Valdez? You feeling okay? You looked pale. Want a glass of water?"

I answered, "I am okay. No problem. Thanks."

Emma continued: "Tessa loved poetry, writing inspirational messages and always dreamed one day of having her book published. She was also a good classical pianist. We truly miss her. I will show you her room, still untouched — exactly as it was before she died. I will also show you all her writings. They are almost identical to yours. Please come inside."

I followed Emma inside. Again, I had a feeling of familiarity with the place as if I had been there all my life.

Her room 'Tessa' was at the far end, the first room near the front door. We entered the bedroom; again the smell, the sights were so close to my senses and heart. Familiarity reigned once more.

Emma handed me a neatly kept file of writings inside an envelope.

Upon reading Tessa's writings, I realised that although different words had been used, meanings, themes, messages were almost identical to mine.

I heard Chris's voice at the verandah saying, "C'mon Evelyn, we have to keep moving. The kids have to be dropped off at their place."

I said, "Okay, Chris."

I kissed and hugged goodbye to Emma and George. Such a lovely couple to lose their only child.

I did not say anything about the connection between Tessa and me.

Emma said, "It was strange, but I could feel I had a good connection with you the moment I saw you."

I said, "Same with me, Emma. Really nice meeting you and for sure this will not be our last time. Hope we will be seeing each other some time."

Emma replied, "Of course. You can visit us anytime and you can bring your grandkids. They are so adorable."

Driving home that afternoon, I was quiet. Chris looked at me and said, "Evelyn, you have not said a word since we left. Anything bothering you?"

I replied, "It's okay. I just feel exhausted after a long day. Nothing to worry about."

But in my mind, now I knew the reason why I was still here — to continue the mission and calling. One day I will be able to explain this to Chris and to the beautiful couple Emma and George. That will be…when the time is right.

There are some things in our lives

That we cannot comprehend or explain

A beautiful moment can always happen

Even if we are not aware of it

And if the time comes when it is there

Don't be scared to follow it

Chase your dreams and most of all

Chase your DESTINY

Chapter IX

Inspirational Messages

1. Mother's Heart

A mother's heart is so strong

It can withstand all the pain

Sorrow and heartaches

Inflicted by loved ones

A mother's heart can still withstand

And forgives no matter what

Even there is no more left to give

One cannot fathom a heart of a mother

Unless you are a mother

Chapter IX

2.

At times the anticipation

Of fear

Is even worse than

The reality itself

3.

Excuses will be made

Reasons will be given

But

To show how you

Care and love someone

You don't need excuses

It should

Be manifested in every way

4.

Be not deceived by

Those who easily weep and cry

By those who look kind and gentle

At times their hearts can be

As cold as ice

Chapter IX

5.

What words failed to say

The eyes say all

Chapter IX

6.

When you gaze yourself at the mirror

Do you see the real you

Or just an illusion and impersonation

Of you

We have all the power to change

It all depends on you

Chapter IX

7.

Just a simple smile

A warm hello and gracious thank you

Would make anyone's day

Very special

8.

One form of revenge

Is not hurting the opponents physically

It's about destroying them

Watching them fall apart

Mentally, emotionally and spiritually

It is even worse than a death sentence

9.

Friendship is like a business partnership

Both people should take responsibility

To nurture, work hard

To make it flourish and grow

10. Mothers

It's in the mother's heart

That children can find

Assurance of being loved

It's in the mother's arms

That children can find

Solace and comfort

But

It's in the mother's hugs and kisses

That the children can find the real joy

Of being loved and most of all

Being special and cared for

Chapter IX

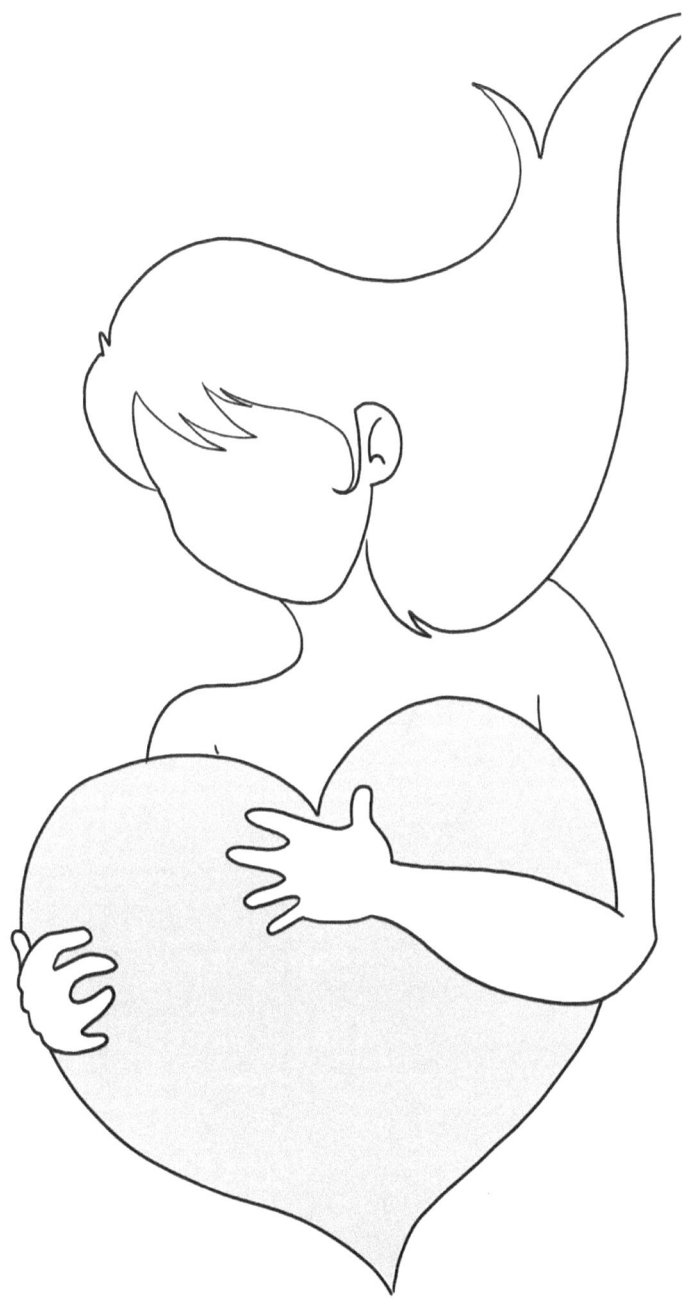

11. **Love**

A universal language

Love encompasses everything

Defies reasons, logic, and

Conquers all along its path

No one can be immune to

Its power, regardless of

Who you are

12.

We always mourn for

The loss of loved ones

But no one mourns

For the loss of one's soul

13.

There are times that it

Is vital

To analyse the past

Before

You can fathom or comprehend

The present and the future

14. Memories

It's a timeless remembrance

Of one's childhood, we all

Shared with friends and families

But then, change within us becomes

Inevitable and unavoidable

We start to drift apart

From all familiar faces, loved ones and friends

We begin to search for the quest of fame and glory

Destroying everything that crosses our path

In order to achieve the success we so desire

Thus at the end upon reaching

The culmination of our success

We still feel miserable, lonely and empty

There is something void within our hearts

That no one can see

Only you can feel

You begin to question it

Is it all worth it?

To lose loved ones and friends

And most of all

Lose your soul?

It's not too late yet. You can change

And turn around your life

It's your choice, it's your decision

It's your life

15.

Your imagination is

The beginning and the stepping stones

For the creation and the

Fulfilment of your dream

16. I believe

As parents:

We make sure that our kids

Will be able to look after themselves

When we are gone

Teach them to be self-reliant

Independent

To be strong yet caring

To be focused, but aware of

Their own limitations

To be sensitive about different issues

Yet to be open minded to everything

We cannot be with them forever

And learning these values our

Kids will be equipped to face

All difficulties in life

17.

It is what we believe and our convictions

That make us who and what we are today

It is what we fight for that

Makes us stronger than ever

And most of all

It is our love and compassion

That can easily open our hearts

So we can help the people who need it most

18.

Reliving the moments

Of once beautiful memories

Can always bring

Sunshine and hope

Especially when one

Is in the middle

Of a personal conflict

19.

Though we are human

We still have the power to choose

To be evil and righteous

To be a success or be a failure

To be miserable or to be happy

To be moral or indecent

To be just or unjust

To be truthful or be deceitful

Whatever you choose

Will determine

Who and what you will be

Now and the future

You should be responsible

For your life

And no one else

20.

At times our ego

Is so much bigger and

Stronger than our conscience

Making us do the unthinkable

Making one's judgments unreasonable

Regardless of who will suffer

At the end

21.

Through the eyes of children

Their parents are their role models and their heroes

Therefore it is the responsibility

Of every parent to set high standards

To be able to produce

Future responsible adults.

 **22.**

Being positive is one

Of the many ways

To face challenges in life

23.

Those who suffered abuse

Had pain and disappointments

In life

Will emerge either as

Stronger souls

Or people full of hatred of vengeance

At the end

Becoming the abusers and

Aggressors themselves

24.

When greed and envy overtake a person

Then you start selling your

Soul to the devil

And it's too late to realise

It is not all worth it

25.

One should always be strong

To follow your beliefs and convictions

Failing to do so

Will haunt you forever

In your life

26. Change

Everything will come to an end

What was relevant before

Does not exist anymore

There will come a time when

You get tired of putting yourself

Last for others

It's time to embrace a new chapter

In your life.

And the only priority in mind

Is looking after oneself

First and foremost

Because nobody will do it for you

But yourself…a time for change

Chapter IX

27.

Truth hurts, but then
Again, you cannot run
Forever from the truth

28.

There are moments that the
Sweetest words to be heard
Are those that are yet unspoken
And still buried in one's heart

29.

May one's life experiences

Be a pathway for perfection

Be an inspiration

To achieve your goals

And the ultimate dreams

Of your life

30.

Treating someone as a person first

Not by what and who they are

Or their status in the community

Nor what they can do for you

Is the noblest act of all

31.

Don't let your generosity

Be against you

At times people can

Manipulate and abuse, use you

For their own benefit

And satisfaction

32.

Perhaps the most agonising

Pain of all

Is the one still deep in your heart

That no one can see or tell

But you are the only one

That can feel and bear

33.

Honesty and being truthful

Begin first in oneself

Before it can fully

Transcend to others

Sounds simple but difficult to do

Especially when one's ego

Will be affected

34.

I wish I could be remembered

Not by whom I was

But by what I was

And the things I did

During my living years

35.

Some people judge you

For what they don't have

Or because of their own inadequacies

At times they rejoice for other's miseries

Abhor others for their

Achievement and success

An ugly side of human behavior

36.

People who pretend too much

Won't know when the fantasy ends

And the reality begins...

37.

At times we can learn

Something

From the innocence, purity,

And unadulterated mind

Of a child

38.

Ode to the lost loved one

Happiness and life together

We once had

Has been taken away from us

All those that we shared

Those precious moments

And precious times that we had

It's now just past memories

It's all that I have

They say time will heal

The pain I feel

But the scar and loneliness

In my heart

Will always be here

That will never take time to heal

39.

It's up to us to relinquish

The past

Then to let it go and move on

Failing to do so

We become a prisoner of ourselves

And peace within

Can never be found

Chapter IX

40.

At times friends can ease

Sorrow and problems

They can be a guiding light

When you see yourself

Falling into pieces

When things go wrong

41.

There is no such thing

As one fits all in shoes

The same with people

Just because others did it

So well and succeeded

Does not mean you can

Do the same

42.

The first thoughts or words

That a person says

Will usually define

Their true character and personality

No matter the effort

Of how they want to change it

It is the subconscious mind

That dictates it

43. *To a husband*

Though the years pass

The stronger bond still exists

Both of us have changed physically

But we have grown stronger together

With a more mature outlook in life

Thus the love for one another

Continues to flow

Regardless of all obstacles

We have endured

As we walk

Through the journey

Of our lives

I am

Proud to have him as my husband

My soul mate

And my real best friend

44.

The impact or aftermath

We feel within

Is more significant

Than the experience

We had

Hence the next step

Will be crucial

And you can be the only one

Who can decide

On which road

Or journey of life to follow

45.

One of the reasons

We abhor others

Is because we can

See through them

Our inner weakness

That others don't have

46.

There are times

We want to leave

Away from our past

But our past never leaves us

Keeps on haunting us

Wherever and whenever we are

And it is up to us to accept

And deal with it courageously

Chapter IX

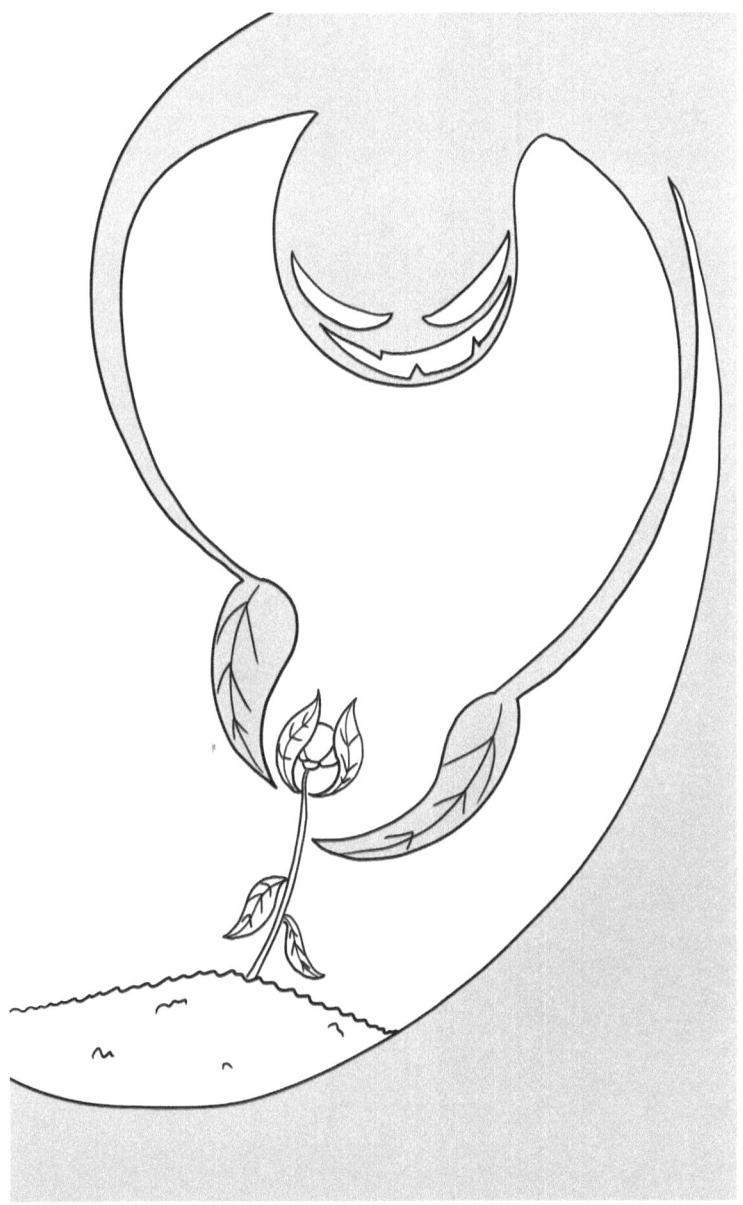

47.

What's wrong with today's world

No one wants to take responsibility

For their actions

Instead they opt for the easy way out

Blaming others

Except themselves

48.

Wondering what tomorrow brings

But anyway I just go on living

Until I reach my goal

Until I can be fully satisfied

That all my dreams will be fulfilled

49.

Once you can see through

The beauty, kindness, and greatness

Of each person

One's inner peace

Can be easily achieved

50. I believe

There is no right or wrong

It's just only a matter of opinion

Depends upon culture beliefs and convictions

—Lorna Ramirez

www.ingramcontent.com/pod-product-compliance
Lightning Source LLC
Chambersburg PA
CBHW031425290426
44110CB00011B/521